EAST AND WEST
TWO VILLAGES, OI

G000275629

BEFORE DOMESDAY

What evidence there is for human activity in Runton before 1086 results mainly from random surface finds of worked flints or sherds of pottery. While there has been no large-scale field-walking and much of the land is now permanently under grass, scatters of Mesolithic and Neolithic tools have been found in the fields between the two villages. Several Paleolithic hand-axes have also been discovered, but the once well-known eoliths are now generally considered to be flints shaped by natural processes.

It is interesting to note that there seems to be a concentration of finds of artefacts in the vicinity of Woman Hithe at West Runton. From the cliff-face came a barrel-shaped pottery vessel of the Bronze Age and a bowl of Rinyo-Clacton grooved ware dating from the Neolithic period, together with two skeletons and pottery of the Iron Age, Romano-British and Medieval periods. A few Roman coins and a gold stater have also been discovered there. This obviously reflects much early activity at a favoured site, but the number of finds may be related to the intensity of wear on the sandy soil of the car park and its surroundings in recent years. From East Runton come two jet rings about 2 inches in diameter, described as pendants dating from the Romano-British period, which are currently on exhibition at the British Museum.

In 1859 a brief and vague account was given of the digging-up of 'several rude black urns filled with burnt bones' from a ploughed field somewhere in Runton. The site and the fate of the urns are now unknown.

The presence of iron slag near the so-called Roman Camp has been known for at least two centuries. In 1883 the site and the surrounding pits known as Hills and Holes were surveyed and slag was found as a component of the earthwork. Yet the idea persisted that the pits had been made for human habitation. Excavation by Dr.R.F.Tylecote in 1964 showed that these were in fact dug to provide the nodules of iron oxide used in a nearby smelting furnace, which could have produced some 50 tons of metal from about 1000 pits. The period during which the bloomery site operated was probably some time between 850 and 1150 AD.

1

EARLY MANORIAL SITUATION

The story is not at all clear from the late 11th to the early 13th century, despite gradually increasing documentation. It is concerned mainly with the break up and the re-assembly of manors and the creation of new ones, and the details remain obscure.

The currently accepted view of the Domesday Book is that in Beeston (Besentuna) two Norman magnates, Hugh de Montfort and William d'Ecouis, each held one ploughland (taken to be about 120 acres): and that in Runton (Runetune) d'Ecouis held another ploughland, while Roger Bigod, Sheriff of Norfolk and Suffolk, had 30 acres. This view ignores the identification by Blomefield of another of de Montfort's holdings, one ploughland in Rugutune, as being at Runton.

It is generally accepted that Beeston Priory was founded about 1216 by Margaret de Cressy and that further benefactions were made by her daughter-in-law, Isabella. Indeed, the latter has also been considered to be the foundress. However, other gifts were made to the Priory after her death in 1263. For example, in December 1279 Margaret, widow of Nicholas de Chostes, made a quitclaim to the Prior and Convent of Beeston renouncing her dower rights in the lands and manorial privileges which her husband had formerly possessed, including ⅕ th of the advowson of Runton church. It may be that the outcome of the re-organisations made in the 13th century is represented approximately by the way in which the profits of 'wreck of sea', i.e. flotsam and jetsam, coming ashore anywhere at Beeston or Runton were shared between the various manors 100 years later. At the end of the 14th century this was usually expressed according to a set formula; 'The lord of Beeston has one half, and of the other half the Prior of Beeston has 3 parts, the lord of Felbrigg has 1½ parts and John de Plumstede has ½ part', from which it is clear that each 'part' is ⅕ th of the second half of the profits.

COASTAL AFFAIRS

There is one thread which runs throughout the story of Runton up to the present day, and that is the continual ravaging of the land by the sea. Professor Keith Clayton has been quoted as saying that the coastline between Weybourne and Happisburgh has been retreating at a rate of about one metre a year for 6000 years. This may not be entirely true of Runton, for some fields which were already suffering erosion in the late 15th century had not yet finally disappeared in 1840 when the Tithe Map was drawn.

It should, however, come as no surprise to learn that Runton has lost a settlement just as Shipden (off Cromer) was lost, although over a longer period of time. In the late 14th century in East Runton there were 11 messuages, four 'howses' (which may not have been dwellings, although one had a well) and two granges situated either in Seagate, as Beach Road or Cliff Lane was then called, or slightly to the West 'by the Sea's Syde'.

The Tithe Map of 1840 shows that there were still six cottages and a wash-house on the cliff-top. The names of owners and occupiers are listed in the Apportionment. An etching by Robert Blake in 1834 shows that some of these buildings were thatched. By the time of the survey made in 1885 for the 1st edition of the 6" Ordnance Survey map all had gone. Another had been built about 100 yards west of the Gap. This, known as Strongarm's Cottage from the nickname of its occupant, also disappeared soon after World War I.

West Runton does not appear to have had any similar settlement. In the late 15th century there were only arable strips beyond the King's meadows at the end of 'Medowe Lane', as Water Lane was then called. It may be to West Runton that Edmund Hook referred in his bequest, in 1723/4, setting up a charity to provide 'fewel for the poor of Beeston and Upper Runton'.

While a survey of the 1490s refers to several pieces of land as having been reduced in size through erosion, the court rolls of the manor of Runton Stubbes illustrate what must have occurred very often. In 1539 Isabella Smythe inherited from her father, Robert Burflete, a cottage and 2½ acres of land. Robert Macke, son of her second marriage, was six years old when the property came to him in 1560, and he was therefore made the ward of his grandmother, Isabell Hillington. In 1564, on his behalf, she sought permission 'to take down, overthrow and draw back a house or cottage because the ebb and flow of the water would prevent its being rebuilt if it were not to be destroyed by the pounding of the waves'. As she paid 40 pence, quite a large sum, for the privilege one must suppose that the building was dismantled and re-erected further inland. Yet, in 1617, after Robert Macke's death had been reported, a marginal note in the court book stated 'the howse and all the land is in the sea saving V roods'.

The records of the various manors do not set out to note maritime affairs, but as 'wreck of sea' was a valued perquisite references to this are often found. In December 1392, at a court of the manor of Beeston-iuxta-Mare, the jurors of East Runton reported that the following had come ashore: '40 barrels, 20 empty, 20 full of beer; 46 planks of oak panelling; one oak tree, part of a ship called 'Le Dele'; one windlass, four spars and two steering oars'. The Beeston jurors also reported the finding of : ' 9 planks of oak panelling; 30 wooden stakes and a small barrel'. A month later the court of Runton Felbrigg's manor met, and referred to what may well have been the same wreck, with the finding of an unspecified number of barrels of beer and '36 boards of oak panelling'. None of these items was valued, a job normally done jointly by the messors, or haywards, of the larger manors involved, but the proceeds were to be divided according to the formula already mentioned.

In February 1588, a Scottish ship returning from France was wrecked near Runton and was looted by Roger Windham of Felbrigg and others. Goods valued at £600 were removed and apparently stored in Runton parsonage, which is assumed to have been ruinous at this period, the rector being non-resident. Next day his brother, Sir Francis Windham, a Justice of Common Pleas, removed a further £700 worth of cargo to the safety of his own house and issued search warrants to the constables of neighbouring villages for the recovery of the loot, but much remained missing.

Many present inhabitants of Runton will recall several instances of ships coming ashore in gales or fog, although happily with modern navigational aids this is almost a thing of the past. On the night of 20th

The 'Gold Crown' ashore at East Runton, with Cromer lifeboat and a tug in attendance, November 1933. (H H Tansley)

November 1933 in dense fog, the motor barge 'Gold Crown', laden with dust coal for Norwich power station, went aground at Wood Point, East Runton, and was not re-floated until nine days later. Part of the cargo was jettisoned and many people from the neighbourhood and farther afield obtained a good supply of free coal, though not without hard work.

A year later on 24th November 1934, a Dutch motor vessel, the 'Rian' of Groningen, bound for London with coal, also went aground, at West Runton this time, in dense daytime fog. Grounded at 10 a.m., she was re-floated at high tide at 7.30 p.m.

The 'Lady Gwynfred' beached at East Runton, November 1936. (H H Tansley)

On 18th November 1936, the sailing barge,' Lady Gwynfred', came ashore near Wood Point, but was eventually re-floated. Continuing the toll of that deadly eleventh month, on 12th November 1937, the 'Hibernia' was less fortunate and broke up on East Runton beach.

Cliff falls and slips continue to gnaw away at the coastline. It is probably over 20 years since Wood Point, itself a low promontory of chalk and clay protruding about 20 feet onto the beach, was finally eroded away. In Savin's History of Cromer, 1936, mention is made of a large glacial boulder, then about 100 yards from the cliff at Goss's Gap. This was reputed to have been at the foot of the cliff in the early 19th century. The inscription it bears is not quite as Savin quoted, but, though greatly battered, consists merely of the initials S C and a date which appears to be 1773. This stone is now seldom visible except at Spring tides.

The remains of the 'Hibernia', November 1937. (H H Tansley)

Finally, mention must be made of the disastrous tidal surge which occurred on the night of 31st January 1953. Contrary to a recent account, East Runton was not flooded, but much damage was caused along the shore, to the cliffs, the sea wall and the public lavatories. Beach huts were smashed and carried away by the violence of the sea and wind. But the boats had all been pulled up the Gangway to safety before the waters reached their full height, when the run of the waves was nearly halfway up the slope and spray came over the cliff.

The stone, marked SC 1773, reputed to have been at the foot of the cliffs in the early 19th century. (G F Leake)

HALF YEAR LANDS

As a consequence of the Commons Registration Act, 1965, a costly enquiry lasting 17 days was held in November 1975 and January 1976, first in Norwich and then in London. Its objectives were to determine what was common land and what rights were connected with it, and, more importantly, what grazing rights existed over the half-year lands. These latter were a carry-over from medieval communal agriculture, where after harvest the unsown arable land lay open for controlled grazing from Michaelmas to Lady Day. There has been no Enclosure Act for Runton, and both the Tithe map of 1840 and the 1st 6" Ordnance Survey map of 1885 reveal considerable evidence of an open-field parish, with many narrow strips of land, some of less than a quarter of an acre, divided only by grass balks. It was principally this area lying outside the core of the two villages, and by now mostly enclosed or amalgamated into larger fields, over which half-year rights were claimed on behalf of the inhabitants of Runton.

In the event, the Commissioner registered all the existing commons, which meant that three small ones shown on the Tithe map, at Deer's Hill and on either side of the road at Oxwell Cross, had been finally lost. He refused to confirm any rights over the commons or over the former half year lands. Regarding the latter, he remarked that the claimed rights had acted as 'a restrictive covenant against the use of half year land for purposes inconsistent with grazing'. So ended a controversy that had continued on and off at least since the end of the last century, and had been marked by the deep and sincere conviction of the claimants in their rights as part of an ancient heritage.

Situated on the northern face of the Cromer-Holt Ridge and its adjoining coastal plain Runton lies in that part of Norfolk where an integrated sheep-corn husbandry was practised during the Middle Ages and long afterwards. The fertility of sandy soil was maintained by the dung of sheep which grazed, or more particularly, were folded on fallow land. Sheep-farming was mainly carried out by manorial lords, whose rights included liberty of foldcourse, or by those to whom their sheep-walks had been let. Each flock was, in theory, confined to its own foldcourse, a well defined area which normally included heaths and commons for Spring and Summer pasture, and arable land, of which the unsown portion provided communal grazing through Autumn and Winter. This arable was the half-year land.

A view of the common at East Runton, taken prior to 1892. (Mrs N M Leake)

Above and opposite: A shepherd with a cullet flock near Incleborough Hill. (Randall/Salter Magic Lantern Slide Collection)

Sheep appear early in the history of Runton. In 1086, d'Ecouis' land carried 60, while de Montfort's holding, to follow Blomefield, had 15. Both estates kept goats rather than sheep at Beeston.

Little evidence survives about conditions before the end of the 14th century. From then on people were frequently fined for causing damage in their neighbours' corn with their sheep and other animals; also for failure to maintain fallgates and fences adjoining the commons.

But already it was apparent that shepherds of the large manorial flocks were not very careful to keep to their own foldcourses. Twice in 1393 the shepherd of Felbrigg Hall, one John Wroughmowgth (surely the nickname of an abusive fellow) was reported to have violated the regulations of the Beeston manor in Runton. His flock had caused damage in the tenants' hay and corn, and had grazed illegally on the commons of that manor.

In the 16th century, Sir Francis Windham, Recorder of Norwich, inherited the Priory manor and leased that of Beeston Regis for £20 a year. An interesting sidelight on this rent is shown in a complaint he brought before the court of the Duchy of Lancaster in 1583. Peter Platten, Clement Wilkinson and Thomas Whynnet, none of them having freehold property worth 40 shillings a year, 'unlawfully kept Ferettes, nettes and other engyns to take Conyes with'. They had taken so many rabbits from his warren and had prevented the warreners from entering their lands that he was experiencing difficulty in raising his annual rent from the estate. Poaching had evidently gone down in the social scale: two centuries earlier the culprits, using dogs, had included local clergy and the famous Sir Thomas Erpingham.

The position on the half-year lands in the 19th century was plainly stated in the sale particulars of the late Rev.Paul Johnson in 1836. 'The half-year lands are subject to Sheep Walks and the Depasture of great and commonable cattle, from the 10th October to the 5th April and the Dole Lands (i.e heaths) are also subject to a Sheep Walk for 400 sheep belonging to Beeston Abbey Farm, from the 5th April to the 10th October, in every year'.

On 26th June 1900 at the Law Courts, Judge Willis declared that 'there had existed in the inhabitants of Runton from time immemorial the rights claimed of pasturage on the Half Year lands' and that this right could

be legally enforced against the persons who owned the lands. He refused, however, to say whether the judgment would be binding in future cases. Following this case the District Council accepted compensation from owners who had infringed the Half Year rights.

Not long after the judgment, Runton Parish Meeting actually voted in favour of abolishing the rights. In 1912, five of the larger property owners applied for a Provisional Enclosure Order, but this was refused.

During the agricultural recession of the inter-war years summer camping sites became popular on land that had been let down to grass. But the great surge came with the increased mobility of people after World War II, when caravan sites sprang up mainly, but not entirely, on the seaward side of the two villages. To avoid any suggestion of contravening the Half Year rights the District Council issued licences which, in effect, respected the period of shackage. It was also appreciated that the restrictions on uses inimical to grazing had retained the rural appearance of the parish.

However, in 1951, when some 18 acres of the 100 year old Fair Lady Plantation were clear felled, there was no replanting because the land could not be enclosed with a fence against rabbits on account of these rights. This was a rather ironic situation since the original plantation must of necessity have been similarly protected. Indeed, one of the first acts of Sir Thomas Fowell Buxton on purchasing the Johnson estate around the end of 1840 was to plant trees on the dole lands and to fence them in. In a letter, dated 25th February 1843, replying to a complaint by William Windham of Felbrigg he acknowledged that this enclosure was 'by sufferance' of other owners who might have rights there. But he totally refused to pay even a nominal sum in compensation so as not to create a precedent.

When the enquiry came the Commissioner's first act was to declare Judge Willis's decision ultra vires and therefore not to be considered. Despite evidence regarding a cullet flock in 1913 under its shepherd, James 'Jimmy Dykey' Abbs, and an Abbey Farm flock which continued until the early 1920s with its own shepherd, 'Spuddy' Shepherd, it was clear to an impartial observer that the rights were as good as lost. So it proved.

One may wonder how it came to be believed that merely inhabiting Runton conferred the right to participate in the cullet flock. The following tentative suggestion is offered. In 1801 the total population of Runton was 312, being 60 households occupying 50 houses. It may well have been less in the 18th century. Most families would need a little land to feed a donkey or horse, possibly a few other domestic animals. As occupants of half year land

Opposite: A reduced version of the first 6" Ordnance Survey map, surveyed in 1885, showing Runton just before the railway was constructed in 1887.

they would be entitled to join the cullet flock; but if most families were in the same position then the distinction between the two capacities, occupiers of land and inhabitants of Runton, may have become blurred. The legal position was given in 1899, but custom is seldom written down, and no code of by-laws seems to exist for any of the manors. We just do not know what transpired during the 17th and 18th centuries to transform what had been a resented privilege of manorial lordship into a cherished right of the inhabitants of Runton.

THE CHURCH AND SOME CHURCHMEN

The intimate connection between Runton and Beeston is exemplified in the case of the church, which stands almost on the parish boundary where it runs over the Mill Hill of the Beeston Regis manor.

In 1086 the church and its 6 acres were included in the measurement of William d'Ecouis' Beeston estate. A survey of the 1490s shows that the two parsonages lay side by side next to Runton church, and that their glebe lands were similarly close together. The same document states that in the case of the first seventeen furlongs listed, mainly in the south-eastern part of East Runton, the tithes of numerous strips, usually belonging to the Crown manor, were payable to Beeston church and not to Runton.

The Tithe maps of the two parishes show that in 1840 the glebe lands of each lay mainly in Runton, and that both there and in Beeston were generally contiguous. So one is left wondering about the origin of these arrangements; whether indeed it goes back beyond the Domesday Book, and whether there was originally one larger parish.

There are references in the late 15th century to a chapel in East Runton. Chapel Lane is noted in the 18th century, and Chapel Lane Close is the name given on the Tithe map for a field where Brick Lane joins Thain's Lane, both of these names being of later date. Faden's map of Norfolk, 1796, appears to call Top Common 'Chapel Green', which has not been found anywhere else. Nothing more is known at present.

It is not proposed to say much about the fabric of the church, a subject covered by the guide and by Pevsner and later writers.

It would seem that the church may not always have been dedicated to the Holy Trinity. Most testators, even before the Reformation, refer only to the parish church of Runton as their chosen place of burial. However, of 40 wills surviving from the period between 1469 and 1561, 14 specifically refer to the church of Our Lady or the Blessed Virgin Mary of Runton. Possibly a change of dedication was made following the reign of Mary I.

Whether or not the church had suffered much damage during the so-called Great Pillage is not precisely known, but it was stated to be in a ruinous condition in December 1554, the year of Mary's marriage to Philip of Spain. At least that was the reason advanced when permission was given for the union of the benefice to Aylmerton for the incumbency of Edmund Windham. However, this may merely have been a ploy to profit one whose precise relationship to Sir Edmund Windham (or Wyndham) is a matter of conjecture. In 1569 both the rectory and the chancel were reported to be in great ruin, and the rector non-resident. How long Windham remained is not clear, for he was a papist.

Runton seems to have been well involved in one of the religious disputes of the late 16th century, a controversy about the wearing of special vestments. At Bishop Scambler's visitation in 1593, eleven charges were raised by one of the churchwardens, Thomas Whynnet, against the rector, William Clapham. He did not read Common Prayer; nor service on Wednesdays and Fridays; he did not wear the surplice as appointed by the book of Common Prayer; he did not catechise, nor bid fasting days; he was not resident upon his parsonage; he was not peaceable; he did not keep the register; he went to harrow, yet the parsonage barn was in ruins; and finally he refused to christen Whynnet's child on the Sabbath.

The rector rebutted these charges. He could not wear a surplice as there was only an old one, very torn. As to the non-christening of the child, Whynnet had refused to let him do so, saying that no knave should baptize his child. The barn had burned down before his institution; and he bestowed a large part of the income of his benefice on repairs to the chancel and the parsonage houses. At Bishop Redman's visitation in 1597 there is no separate entry for Runton, so presumably Clapham conformed, at least where his spiritual duties were concerned.

However, his will made in 1603 shows that he remained an extreme Protestant, indeed a Calvinist. It is a very long and detailed document in which Clapham made many charitable bequests, both locally and in his native Yorkshire. Among other items it set up a bursary for a poor scholar from Giggleswick School to enter Cambridge University, and established an almshouse and supporting charity in Runton. One small bequest which might at first seem almost blasphemous must be viewed in the light of the religious situation of the times; 'to the Townsmen and Wyves of Runton 20 shillings to make them merry withall in lent next after my death'. To one of Clapham's persuasion anything, such as ritualised grief, that smacked of Rome would have have been anathema.

It was after all only 15 years since the Spanish Armada had threatened the kingdom. Clergy, just as laymen, had to show a certain amount of armour at musters of the Militia. While it is probable that Clapham's store may have belonged to his wife's first husband the list is quite impressive. The inventory

A lithograph by Ladbroke, showing Runton church in the 1820s.

of his goods and chattels, valued at 624 5s 4d, included : in the study, 'two calivers (light muskets), two musketts, one fully furnyshed, one fowling peece, a Curate (cuirass or body armour) furnyshed, one staffe, one blacke bill, two brush hooks, one old pistoll, two longe bowes, one stone bowe, two scottishe Daggers, two swords, two daggers, one gauntlet and one half pyke', and in the low combe (dormer) chamber, 'a sheiffe of arrowes'. Similarly, Clapham's successor, William Flemynge, later rector of Beeston as well, left in his effects, one Corslett (body armour) furnyshed'.

In 1622 John Furmary was insituted rector of both Beeston and Runton. A Royalist, he was removed from his cure during the Civil War, and when he made his will in September 1643 was a prisoner in Buckenham Castle. Presumably he was not then held very long because the Committee for Plundered Ministers in February 1646/7 deferred hearing his case until May on account of his age and inability to travel to London in winter. He had, however, already been termed the late rector. It seems likely that Furmary was re-instated at the Restoration of 1660, since his will was not proved until 15th June 1661. A new rector, Roger Flint, was presented by John Windham, the patron, at the end of June and instituted a month later. According to Blomefield, Flint, another Royalist, had been ejected from three benefices during the Commonwealth period.

In 1648, during Furmary's enforced absence, Edward Worsley, brother of one of Cromwell's major-generals, became rector of the two parishes, and after the Restoration, was appointed to the living at Letheringsett. Two of his letters to his father have been published and shed some light on the harshness of conditions. In April 1649 he wrote of the very high price of corn, with wheat and rye at twice the normal rate. In February 1650/1, he complained of government charges and taxes being much greater than previously, with money scarce and the return on corn 'indifferent'. His last

14

two month's tax assessment had been more than £3, while the corn merchant with whom he dealt had failed and decamped, owing the rector over £5.

Following all the ferment of the 16th and 17th centuries the church at Runton seems to have slumbered and slowly decayed. In the 19th century much needed repairs were carried out, but the result was the the loss of some of the remaining medieval character including the lower half of the screen. William Clapham had left £10 for the erection, on the north side of the chancel door, of a tomb three feet high to house his leaden coffin. Such a tomb, with the brass missing, apparently existed on the north side of the chancel in the early 19th century, but is now no more.

As may be seen from Ladbrooke's lithograph, executed before 1825, there were formerly four clerestory windows on the south side of the nave. The scars resulting from the removal of two buttresses supporting the wall of the south aisle can still be seen. Whether a second small perpendicular window there was uncovered or inserted is unclear. Perhaps the artist's recording is at fault. The opening-up of the large perpendicular windows in the chancel to their full height must have vastly improved the internal lighting. The north porch, in ruins in 1840, was converted into a vestry.

The rising tide of Non-Conformity in the 19th century brought about the building of a Primitive Methodist chapel at East Runton in 1845. This was enlarged in 1897 by the construction of the present chapel, which retained half of the original as a school-room. The Methodist chapel at West Runton, replacing a wooden building, was erected in 1951 as a memorial to Willie Long, fisherman-evangelist, a lay preacher widely known and respected in fishing ports.

Runton church, 1987. In most respects it matches the Ladbroke lithograph, except for the buttresses and clerestory windows. (G F Leake)

West Runton, April 1981. Relatively recently constructed defences are seen at the foot of the cliffs, but we can imagine considerably more land to the north of the village in the medieval era. (Poppyland Photos)

In July 1958 Runton school closed. The owners, successors to the Buxtons, agreed to sell the buildings to the Parochial Church Council for conversion to a church, which would replace a wooden hut of Army type situated at the other end of Lower Common. On 6th August 1959 St.Andrew's Church was dedicated. But after only a few years, the escalating costs of maintaining a century-old building became too great and the major part was auctioned off, leaving only the former infants' room and lobby as the church. With hindsight, one may feel that a great opportunity was lost at the outset. What might have been a very fine multi-purpose hall, accommodating both secular and religious functions as the school had often done in its time, has been lost to the village as a public asset. All that remains for the public is the rump of the building together with a small, very utilitarian village hall occupying the former school gardens. A minor tragedy.

THE COMMUNITY: PEOPLE AND TAXES

Most figures for population before the first Census in 1801, whose accuracy has sometimes been doubted, are of necessity 'guesstimates', involving the application of some theoretical multiplier to lists made for some other purpose, usually taxation.

If one accepts Blomefield's view of the holdings in 1086, there were 44 men, possibly heads of households. Under Roger Bigot were 2 freemen, 5 villeins and 2 bordars; under William d'Ecouis 10 bordars and 5 socmen; and

A general view looking down towards West Runton in the first decade of the century. (Poppyland Collection)

under Hugh de Montfort 12 bordars and 8 socmen. However, if the last holding is taken to have been in Roughton, then the total is only 24

Walter Rye, the 19th century antiquarian, published two Subsidy Rolls for the early years of the reign of Edward III. In 1327, 37 people, mainly men, paid 57 shillings. This list includes William Haye, posibly the last manorial lord actually to reside in the vill. In 1332, 38 persons paid 60 shillings and 2 pence. From 1334 the figure was fixed at an arbitrary sum of 66 shillings and 2 pence, until 1449 when a reduction of 10 shillings was made on account of impoverishment.

Some clue as to the severity of the Black Death in Runton may be gained from the court rolls of Runton Hayes manor. On 17th February 1348/9 a court was held for Robert de Reppes. The next one was held nine months later, on 19th November 1349, on behalf of his widow, Dame Alice. It dealt with land transfers resulting from the recent deaths of 21 tenants, male and female, many of whose surnames appear on the earlier Subsidy Rolls. As Runton Hayes was one of the smaller manors, with around 10% of the land, the death toll for the whole vill must have been considerably greater, although it is recognized that some people may have held land from more than one manor as they did at the end of the 14th century.

In the early part of the reign of Richard II Runton was affected, like most of Norfolk, by the unrest precipitated by fresh Poll Tax demands and which culminated in the so-called Peasants' Revolt of 1381. One of the objects of this Rising of the Commons, as it was then termed, was the destruction of manorial archives which recorded among other things a person's status, bond or free, and obligations in rent and services. Few local documents survive from earlier periods, but the court rolls of Runton Hayes, in a somewhat broken series from 1281, record nothing special during 1381 or the next few years. The rolls for Beeston-iuxta-Mare (later Regis) do not commence until 1384, which may imply destruction of the records. However, those of Runton Felbrigg's begin in October 1381 with a heading stating that this was the first court held since the burning of the manorial archives 'by the Commons of the Country'. A certain amount of passive disobedience is noted, such as refusal to perform labour services. One man, however, had made his own demonstration of disaffection. Robert Bully was a villein tenant of the Beeston manor, in whose court he came to hold minor office, but he also held land of Runton Felbrigg's. He had driven his horses, cows and sheep to and fro over demesne land of the latter at Holgate 'so reducing to nothing the corn growing there' that barley estimated at 1 quarter 4 bushels and worth 3 shillings and 6 pence was destroyed. He was also fined a similar amount for making an unlawful track there.

At present, conditions during the 15th century remain unclear, but a survey of Runton relating to the 1490s does shed some light on the subject. From this field-book it appears that there were then about 81 dwellings, including the adjoining parsonages of Runton and Beeston, together with two or three houses in ruins. Rentals for two of the manors at the end of the 16th century showed a net increase of 8 dwellings on their lands, while 16 others were in ruins or had been absorbed into larger houses.This would suggest a possibility of around 100 houses at that time. However, in 1603 the ecclesiastical Return of Communicants, presumably all persons over 16, numbered only 153.

Some 70 years later two other returns are no easier to correlate. In 1676, the Compton religious census gives 80 as the number of communicants, there being no non-conformists or papists. The Hearth Tax returns for this period which list the number of fireplaces per house are not well preserved. Using a conflation of several figures J.H.C.Patten showed that in 1674 there were 17 taxpayers and between 43 and 51 poor persons, say 60 to 68 households.

The earliest, and badly kept, parish register for Runton commences in 1742. From that time until the first Census of 1801 baptisms exceeded burials by about 250. The actual increase in population would, of course, have been much less than this, for allowance has to be made for probable emigration, whether within Britain or abroad, for loss at sea of fishermen and other mariners, and also for the likely absence of men in the long Napoleonic War. In view of this increase, the 1801 figure of 312 persons, comprising 60 households living in 50 houses, one other being vacant, seems to imply that the population had dwindled to a very small size by the middle of the 18th century.

In 1765, a return of those eligible for service in the Militia was required. All men between 18 and 45 years of age were to be listed, except certain categories of office-holder, sea-farers and such poor men as had three legitimate children. In the event, 20 names were given, 2 being over age and 5 coming within the various exceptions, so that only 13 able-bodied men were left as eligible.

To return to the 16th century, the scope of the tax known as the Lay Subsidy was widened in the 1520s. In the return for 1524/5, 45 people were assessed, at a total of £3.3.6d. The only trade mentioned is that of ship-wright, represented by Peter and John Platting. The number of taxpayers declined in subsequent years until only 5 men had to raise £3 in 1551/2.

During the first quarter of the 17th century there were official reports of the presence of Dunkirkers off the coast of East Anglia harassing the local shipping with acts of piracy and privateering. An interesting document in the Norfolk Record Office is entitled 'This booke doth shewe what some every severall Corporacion or parishe or towne within the county of Norffolke was rated unto the furnishinge of the first Shippe of war 1635'. This refers to the hated tax, Ship Money. Interestingly, Runton was assessed at £7.3s.6d., Beeston at £3.19s.6d., Sheringham at £7.19s.0d., but Cromer at only £4.4s.8d. The really wealthy places in the Hundred of North Erpingham were Northrepps and Southrepps, each rated at over £18. During the herring season that year there were said to be 1000 Dutch sail off the Norfolk coast.

Harvests were poor in Norfolk during the 1620s, while in 1640, the Sheriff of Norfolk, Sir Thomas Windham, reported 'a general damp of industry'. The poverty of the time is illustrated by a rental of Runton Stubbes manor for 1645. In two cases copyhold land which should have descended by inheritance was 'now letten to fearme (i.e.leased) by reason there would not any come to take them upp because the fine (i.e.entry premium) and charges come to soe much'.

Reminders of external dangers, from the Dutch, are to be found in the Order Books of the Norfolk Quarter Sessions from 1650 onwards. In January 1652, it was ordered that all beacons in the county were to be maintained and watched, as indeed they had been in the 1620s. For the repair and watching of those at Trimingham and Runton, £10 was to be raised in the Hundreds of Mitford and North and South Erpingham. Next year they were each watched at night by one man paid 6d. a night, the county having to raise £200 in respect of 12 beacons.

Where was the Runton beacon? It seems to have been liable to fall quickly into disuse and disrepair. Human memory being what it is, the comments of M.J.Armstrong in his History of Norfolk, 1781, should come as no surprise. Referring to a small ruined building about half a mile north of Aylmerton church, called the Iron Beacon from the material of its construction, he wrote 'At this momentous crisis, when an invasion of our country is threatened by the House of Bourbon, this building, if properly supplied, would be an excellent alarm-beacon, if occasion required'.

There is little doubt that this is what is now called the Roman Camp, in the banks of which iron slag is found as a component. The modern name is believed to have been coined around the turn of the 19th century by a horse-cab driver as a suitably romantic destination for an afternoon's drive.

The site is near what was, at 329 feet, regarded the highest point in Norfolk, until metrication of the Ordnance Survey maps demoted it to second place, below Pigg's Grave near Melton Constable. Such a prominent position may well have been used for the same purpose by the Romans, but real proof of that is lacking.

Maps from the turn of the 18th century onwards show it for what it was. Thus Faden, 1797, terms it Old Beacon or Watch Tower. Bryant, 1826. marks it as Telegraph Station. The first 1" Ordnance Survey map, 1838, calls it Signal Station and shows it standing on Black Beacon Hills. The unpublished 2" drawing prepared for the Ordnance Survey in 1816 labels it Runton Signal House; others being sited at Trimingham and on Kelling Heath. Runton Tithe map, 1840, locates it on Telegraph Dole,while the first 6" Ordnance Survey map, prepared in 1885, marks it simply as Beacon Hill.

It seems likely, then, that the banks visible today are the remains of a signal station dating from the Napoleonic War, part of a chain running along the South and East Coasts from Devon up to Edinburgh. Those from Norfolk downwards were ordered to be 'broken up' in November 1814, but those in the South and South-East were re-activated the next year. Both the Tithe map and the first 1" ordnance Survey map show a 'Gun House', situated in the open fields north of the coast road near Wet Acre. Possibly this also may have been a relic of the French Wars, for its position could command Woman Hithe and Goss's Gap, just as the battery on the Marram Hills at Cromer no doubt commanded East Runton Gap and the approach to Cromer itself.

THE 19TH CENTURY AND LATER

That event of the 19th century which had the most lasting impact on Runton was undoubtedly the purchase of the estate of the late Rev. Paul Johnson by Buxton 'the Liberator'. Sir Thomas Fowell Buxton, Bart. of Bellfield, co. Dorset and Runton, co. Norfolk, died only five years after this acquisition, but he had begun a process of development which was continued by his descendants. The evidence of this is still clearly to be seen.

Familiar with the parish through long enjoyment of shooting rights here and in the neighbourhood, he had previously owned only a few acres. Now in late 1840 or early 1841, by the purchase of some 475 acres he instantly became the major landowner, and with his successors continued to acquire more land. During his last few years, Sir Fowell, as he was usually called, continued, when in Norfolk, to reside at Northrepps Hall, which he had rented since 1828, but set up model farms at Trimingham and Runton. Here he established a sporting estate, his game-keeper being the Irishman, Larry Banville. He made coverts and plantations, giving at least two of them, Fernando (Po) and Niger, names connected with his work for the Abolition of Slavery.

As noted elsewhere, Buxton was unapologetic about fencing in the dole-lands. The attitude of the commoners towards this is not known. It may be that any objection to possible loss of ancient rights was outweighed by sheer necessity. The new woods provided much-needed work in that bitter decade known as the Hungry Forties.

It may now be appropriate to introduce a little oral tradition about conditions in the 19th century. There has long been a rather unlikely tale handed down in the writer's family. James Leake was a blacksmith and a bare knuckle fighter of local repute. The Tithe survey shows that he lived in one of six houses on the cliff at East Runton in 1840, while White's Directory of 1845 states that his forge was at West Runton. The story goes that he had a toe which was either gangrenous or in danger of becoming so. In desperation he put his foot on the anvil, took a chisel and cut off the toe, cauterizing the stump with a red-hot iron.

Corroboration of this improbable story has been provided by 'The Banville Diaries' which quoted a report in the Norwich Mercury of 24th February 1827. Apparently the blacksmith, being unable to afford a surgeon's fees, had coolly made a special implement with which to perform the operation himself. It seems that everything went well, for he continued his prize-fighting, and lived to be 82.

Other, less dramatic, strands of family tradition relate to Oxwell Cross. At one time, drinking water was brought by cart from the spring there and sold in East Runton at a farthing a pailful. This spring served as a place of refreshment for workers in the harvest-fields nearby and also for bearers carrying the dead for burial in the parish churchyard. Apparently it was the men's custom to stop at Oxwell Cross and place the coffin under a rough shelter that stood on the little common on the south side of the road, while

A beach scene entitled 'Runton near Cromer', painted by James Stark and dated 1834. It is difficult to give a precise location for the painting.

Two views of East Runton gap in the 1880s. Both East and West Runton gaps have been used as fishing bases over the centuries, and a small number of boats continue to use them.

they slaked their thirst from the pure, but very cold, water of the spring on the other side. This may, indeed, be an unconscious echo of pre-Reformation custom, since a survey of the 1490s locates the actual cross in a small plot of land on the south side of the place to which it had given its name.

While the Tithe Apportionment of 1840 makes no reference to a school, both the Census of 1841 and White's Directory of 1845 mention a schoolmistress, though not the same person. Some sort of dame-school may have been involved. The cottage next to the Old Hall is said to been used for that purpose at one time.

Whether the Buxtons were involved in education from the beginning of their period in Runton, is unclear, but the second baronet, Sir Edward North Buxton, in 1852 built a school-room on land adjoining Lower Common, East Runton. In the year of his death, 1858, a larger Gothic-style building was erected at right angles to the the first room. Education was conducted according to the principles of the National Society for the Education of the Poor. A further extension, on the north side of the second room was built in 1911.

For more than 80 years the Buxton family, having considerably enlarged its original estate, was the dominating influence in Runton. Besides the school, a men's reading room, to which a billiard room was later added, was provided in East Runton, as well as a fishermen's shelter near the Gangway. Sir E.N.Buxton was closely concerned in the restoration of the church in the 1850s. So firmly indeed was the family associated with the parish that a piece of W.H. Goss's crested china, labelled 'The Manor of Runton', actually bears the Buxton arms.

The Buxton arms appear on this piece of Goss china. (G F Leake)

25

The house which later became a Buxton residence in Runton is called Wright's Farm in the 1841 Census, and Peartree Farm in Directories of 1868 and 1869, the name Runton Old Hall not appearing until 1875. In 1910/11, the building was extensively re-modelled and enlarged for Bertram Hawker who had married into the family. The architect was Bailie Scott; while Gertrude Jekyll laid out the gardens. To facilitate the alterations, a road diversion was necessary. In 1909, Brick Kiln Lane which varied in width from 12 to 18 feet and ran close to the western side of the house, was stopped up for a length of 160 yards. It was replaced by the present road, 18 feet wide including a path, running diagonally for 235 yards to a point near the Brick Works. This was properly called New Road, but that name has been forgotten, the whole now being just Brick Lane.

In the application for the road diversion no mention was made of advantages accruing to the owners of the Old Hall, but only of the benefits to the inhabitants of village, most of whom were said to live to the north and north-east of the site. Traffic from Felbrigg would be saved 4 yards, while that from the northern part of East Runton would have 72 yards less to travel! The year 1909 also saw the completion of the sewerage system in East Runton, which may have been not unrelated to the other work.

However, the people of Runton must by now have become used to gigantic alterations to their familiar surroundings. They had seen gangs of 'navigators' dig the cuttings and make the embankments of the railway line from Holt to Cromer which was inaugurated on 16th June 1887. West Runton station was opened in September of that year. Then, on 23rd July

The Links Hotel and the golf links, separated from West Runton village by the railway line.(Poppyland Collection)

Runton scholars, about 1930. (H H Tansley)

1906, the Runton West-Newstead Lane junction, with an even higher embankment and a five-span bridge, was put to work, so completing the triangle that carves up East Runton. This last link was closed on 21st April 1963, leaving the viaduct as a monument in a conservation area.

The coming of the railway caused changes in the parish, stimulating building as its promoters no doubt intended. Fifty years after the first census the number of inhabitants had risen from 312 to 485, and the houses from 51 to 112, a dozen of these since 1841. For the next thirty years the population rose and fell, being 506 in 1881 when there were 118 dwellings. In 1891, four years after the coming of the railway, there were 601 people and 141 house, with 8 more under construction. Corresponding figures for 1901 were: 840 people and 199 houses, of which 13 were vacant, while 5 more were being built.

The progress of these building surges can be seen today. At West Runton several houses bear the date 1847, while others were built in 1891, notably the imposing Runton House, which replaced what had formerly been Beeston Rectory. The Links Hotel has a plaque dated 1899. At East Runton, with no station of its own, the tendency seems to have been to absorb the overflow of Cromer's holiday trade. From this period there are several terraces of houses built either expressly for boarding visitors or readily adaptable for the purpose. Further expansion took place at West Runton in the 1920s, when shops were built on the south side of the Street.

It is rather surprising to find that the Village Inn was not opened until 9th September 1927, for even in medieval times West Runton had at least two ale-houses. At East Runton, the Fishing Boat has a much longer history. As the Boat Public House it appears on the Tithe map of 1840, and it was in it that the manorial court of Runton Stubbes met in 1816. In 1734 this court was held at the Three Horse Shoes, which may have been an earlier name. The White Horse seems to date from 1851, when the court book of Beeston Priory manor records that Ambrose Mayes sold to William Primrose, brewer, of Trunch, '21 perches of land on which a messuage or dwelling house and other buildings have lately been erected and built'. In September that year Primrose was admitted, as tenant of the manor, to 'a messuage or Public House called the White Horse and other edifices on the same piece'.

CHARITY

It is generally assumed that before the Reformation the relief of the poor and needy was performed by religious establishments such as monasteries. How far this is true of Beeston Priory is not known, but other religious houses which held manors were not particularly benevolent towards their tenants. However, in the last twenty years before the Dissolution one finds two of the priors and a senior canon acting as witnesses, executors or supervisors of the wills of local testators.

Of about 30 pre-Reformation wills of people having ties with Runton, practically all made bequests towards the maintenance of the church. 24 left small sums to one or more of the three gilds there, those of Our Lady, St. Anne and St. John the Baptist; and 11 to the Plough Light.

The Plough Light may, indeed, be remembered in the name of the Ploughlet Charity, which is usually distributed early in the New Year.

In 1603, the Rector of Runton for twenty years, William Clapham, died and by his will, a fascinating document making numerous charitable bequests both in Norfolk and his native Yorkshire, founded a charity to maintain an almshouse. To his executors he left 'my howse in east Runton with the landes thereto belonging which I purchased of William Dingle to thend & purpose that the same shall remaine & be for ever to the use of the Towne of Runton aforesaid for the placeing inhabiting & relieving of two poore folkes be they single or coopled'.

In 1713, Robert Feazer of West Runton, by his will, left 2 acres on the cliff at East Runton in trust to his son and son-in-law, subject to the following condition. On 1st January every year they should distribute the clear yearly rent amongst the 'poor widows and old maids of East and West Runton not taking alms of the said parish'.

In November 1783, James Everett, mariner, and his wife, Elizabeth, gave a cottage with its appurtenances for use by the Churchwardens and Overseers of the Poor of East Runton as a dwelling for the poor of the parish.

This cottage, or its replacement, still stands on Top Common.

From the late 17th to the early 19th century, the trustees, churchwardens and overseers of the poor were drawn mainly from a small grouping of locally influential families, Smith, Goss, Woodrow, Johnson, gentlemen, with one or two of the more substantial farmers, Feazer, Beales, Pank, Breese. They appear not always to have been as correct and assiduous in their unpaid duties as might have been desired. The Rev. Paul Johnson, senior, rector of Beeston Regis, owned probably the largest estate in Runton and lived in what is now Incleborough House. The oddly-shaped extension of the grounds of this house into Lower Common is in fact an encroachment for which he was presented at a court of Beeston Regis manor on 16th November 1808. The enclosure was estimated at one and a half roods, for making which he was fined 2s.6d. He was ordered to restore the land to its former state by 6th April 1809 on pain of forfeiting 40s. No further reference to this occurs in the record. Local tradition, however, has it that land at Sparrow's Park was given in exchange, but documentary evidence has so far proved elusive.

PLACE NAMES

The number of places, lanes, greens, hills and other topographical features that can be traced by name back to the Middle Ages is very small indeed. The Tithe map of 1840, the earliest large scale map of the parish, is of little help because most of its names seem to be of relatively recent origin, bearing little relation to contemporaneous records in manor court books, which generally perpetuate the names of long-dead occupiers and obsolete descriptions. It has proved almost impossible to correlate with the Tithe map a detailed survey of the furlongs and strips of land which made up the field system of Runton in the late 15th century. This is not really surprising in view of an endorsement made on the Beeston glebe terrier (list of lands with which the church was endowed) in 1777. This was to the effect that the ancient descriptions had been repeated because the signatories did not know the exact boundaries, 'many Mier Baulks having been from time to time ploughed up and destroyed'.

Holgate (1382), Oxwell Crosse, Pothill and Woman Hythe Gappe (all late 15th century) are among the names to come through unchanged, although Woman Hithe furlong adjoined Pot Hill and so may properly relate to Goss's Gap before the sea had claimed so much land. Still recognizable from the 1490s are : Wynkyllborow, or Wynkelburgh,for Incleborough Hill; Colgryme (and Colgrim,1603) for Congham Hill; Curres Well for Calves Well; while le Hyrne is noted in 1538. Seagate (1382) in various forms, is Beach Road, formerly Cliff Lane, in East Runton, Medowe Lane in West Runton is

The railway viaduct provided a camera position for this picture of East Runton early in the century. (Poppyland Collection)

now Water Lane. Churchegate Streete (1490s) in West Runton is self-evident.

The various greens and commons seem to have changed names fairly frequently. The Common of West Runton was usually referred to as such, although it may perhaps have been called Westgate Grene (1501) or Kirkegate Grene. At East Runton, South Grene and Kergate Grene are noted in the late 14th century and Bennett's Green in the 16th, but these have not yet been placed. Certainly Top Common was referred to as East Runton Grene in 1521, but occurs in 1552 as Reyman's Grene alias Netillgrene alias Kartegate Grene, while Faden's map of 1797 appears to call it Chapel Green. The 1841 Census terms it Wright's Common. Lower Common may have been Corgate (or perhaps Kergate) Green.

It is probable that the main road, or King's Highway, between East and West Runton ran via Thain's Lane (a recent name) to Incleborough Hill and thence towards the church. What is now the coast road was in the late 15th century merely a common way from each village to Oxwell Cross.

Even on the Tithe map, the Holt road leaving Cromer and forming part of Runton's south-east boundary was still known as Cuckoo Lane. Spelt Cuckow in the 18th century, this name probably derives from a hill, Guckehowgh (1490s), where several closes called Guckhow in the late 16th century had also become Cuckow in the mid-18th. The name may perhaps be recalled in the woodland, Swacking Cuckoo, which lies on the Cromer-Felbrigg boundary just south of the Holt road.

As a name Wood Hill may not be much earlier than the 19th century, but recalls Runton Wood, which probably stood on land long since washed away. In February 1605/6, surveyors acting for James ʰ, as Duke of Lancaster, reported on all the woodland in the 'Manor of Beeston alias Beeston Regis iuxta Mare', which had recently been granted to Thomas Heriott and John Shelbury. Measured in the woodland manner at 18 feet to the pole rather than the normal 16 feet, this consisted of 12 acres of small sapling oaks whose growth was 'greatlye hindered, with the salt water of the mayne Sea, Continually beatinge uppon the same grownde and hath eaten and consumed awaye parte of the grownde thereof'. Wood Point as mentioned elsewhere, disappeared soon after World War II.

INDUSTRY

Apart from the previously-mentioned iron production on the heath near the 'Roman Camp', and perhaps near Incleborough Hill, there has been little industrial activity in Runton. Yet small-scale industrial processes have been carried out here, even though the evidence has largely disappeared or has been removed.

Retting pits - for soaking the fibres of hemp or flax are mentioned as being at the northern end of West Runton Common in 16th century manor

Runton mill in a photograph dating from the late 19th century. (G F Leake)

court rolls. There was also a reference in the 1490's to 'an holde lyme kill' at Marl Pit lands not far from Oxwell Cross. Within living memory there were the remains of another old lime kiln near the Old Butts close to Woman Hithe.

With lime being burnt to provide mortar, bricks also were made locally. Faden's map of 1797 shows a brickground on Brick Kiln Lane in East Runton, where the works were closed in the late 1940s and demolished around 1950. The squat conical kiln was of the brick-bar type and had a capacity of 38,000 bricks, producing in its time tiles and both white and red bricks. A similar kiln with a capacity of 32,000 bricks was operated at Oxwell Cross from 1904 to 1939. This also was demolished after World War II.

In about 1899 new Cromer Gas Works were built just inside the Runton boundary at a point convenient for a rail siding where coal could be brought in and by-products taken out. Rendered redundant by modern pipe-lining techniques which first brought manufactured gas from Norwich and later natural gas from Bacton, even the gas-holders - one only completed in the mid-1950s — have now gone.

What is probably the last traditional herring-house at Runton to retain its internal fixtures is situated on the Lower Common, but has long been used simply as an outhouse.

The only prominent industrial relic is the derelict tower mill at East Runton. While there are references to windmills in the Middle Ages their sites are not precisely known, for wooden post-mills leave little trace when they decay. There is, however, at West Runton the Mill Hill on which part of Runton Hill School stands, but this seems to have been arable land at the end of the 15th century. At East Runton, Mill Hill is the one in the middle of the triangle formed by the railway embankments. No mill is shown on Faden's map, and the present tower is thought to date from the early 19th century. Last worked in about 1908, the mill had a cap of the Norfolk type which rather resembled a clinker-built boat with square bow and stern. The last remaining woodwork of this was removed shortly after the last war on the grounds of safety.

CONCLUSION

It is hoped that this first, tentative, account of some of Runton's past may have been of interest, in spite of its lack of continuity. With luck some of the gaps, whether due to ignorance, lack of material or any other reason, may be filled in by further work, for research into local history is a continuous process, albeit a very slow one. The writer would welcome further information and comments on, or corrections of, this effort.